The EARL

The EARLY DAYS *of* GRIEVING

Derek Nuttall

DARTON · LONGMAN + TODD

Published in 2006 by
Darton, Longman and Todd Ltd
1 Spencer Court
140–142 Wandsworth High Street
London SW18 4JJ

First published in 2001 by Beaconsfield Publishers Ltd.
This revised and updated edition published in 2006
© 2006 Derek Nuttall

The right of Derek Nuttall to be identified as the author
of this work has been asserted in accordance with the
Copyright, Designs and Patents Act 1998.

ISBN 0–232–52644–3

A catalogue record for this book is available from the British Library.

Designed and produced by Sandie Boccacci
Set in 9/12.25pt Arrus
Printed and bound in Great Britain by
Cox & Wyman

Contents

Introduction

This book is offered as a help in the early days of grieving. Grief is not a definite pattern which everyone follows in the same way, so you may not want to read the whole book at once, or you may come across something that seems not to have any relevance at the time, but later it is likely to have some meaning for you. The contents list will help you find comments on particular subjects.

Your family and friends may be unsure how best to help and it may be useful for them to read this as well. Healthcare professionals and bereavement counsellors may also find it helpful.

If you feel you need help do not hesitate to get in touch with one of the organisations listed at the end of the book. They have a lot of experience in helping bereaved people.

1 THE FIRST DAYS

I can't believe it

The death of someone you love is a shattering blow. It is hard to take in even when expected. The shock can be particularly severe when the death is sudden or of someone young. Everything seems unreal and you feel numb. In your early shock you may find you are reacting to people and events in ways that seem unlike you.

What's happening to me?

As the numbness wears off painful feelings can be intense. You may start to think it will always be like this and become panicky. It may seem no one understands and that you are the only person behaving in this way. Longing for the one who is no longer there you go over the past again and again, searching for answers, some meaning and security in what has become a frightening world. Your life has been over-turned. You have lost someone very important and things cannot be the same again. You are grieving and it is natural and understandable to feel the way you do.

How long will it go on?

Facing the reality of your loss will take time and you will go on living for a while as if the person is still here. That has been the pattern of your life and you cannot change it quickly. Grief is like a journey. There will be times when you do not seem to be making any progress but gradually

11

you do move forward. It is not easy. You have suffered a severe loss and you need to give yourself time to cope and recover and to believe that slowly you will work through.

Be prepared for changes in your feelings and responses as time goes by. At first there is the shock and a sense of emptiness. Later there may be pining for the one no longer there, restlessness, questioning, and pain as if an anaesthetic has worn off. Most bereaved people go through very low periods. All this takes place over several months and feelings do not occur in a set order. Try to accept your emotions and reactions as natural.

Expected death

Part of coping with bereavement lies in whether or not we knew it was going to happen.

If you have lost someone who you knew was going to die because of the seriousness of their illness or advancing age you may have begun a kind of grieving before the death came. Some kind of preparation was going on though not necessarily in a conscious way.

It may be that the one who has died was able to talk openly and calmly about what was happening as they neared the end of their life, including thoughts about their personal faith and what they believed happened after death. They may also have given you helpful suggestions about the funeral and their possessions. It could have been a way of helping prepare themselves and you for when death came. You may have felt some upset at this personal sharing but in a way part of the foundation of your recovery in bereavement was being laid by it. Amid all the sadness you may also have comforting memories of the way your loved one faced their death.

Someone dying without warning, giving them and you no time to prepare, can lead to a deeper sense of shock and often takes longer to accept. If there was no chance to say goodbye, share final thoughts or maybe make peace between you, some things can feel unfinished. Although not the same as sharing things before death there are ways of helping you deal with this, including writing a letter to the one who has died putting down everything you wanted to say and wished you had said. It is not for giving to anyone and you may not want to keep it but it can be a way of helping dealing with what seems to be unfinished business.

So too can finding a place where you can be alone and saying things out loud. You are not being morbid or silly if you do this. You are catching up with what death has rushed away, completing a part of what could not be done earlier. It may be painful but it can also be helpful.

If there was some anticipation of the death you may have heard it in a sensitive and patient way from someone in the medical team that gave you time to begin to absorb what was being said and to ask questions. You may have heard it from a relative or friend who stayed with you as you tried to grasp the news. If you were told quietly and caringly that can help you when you go over things in your mind. If the news was broken abruptly or seemingly without awareness of the crucial importance of what was being said it may nag at you and be difficult to lay aside. Like so many other things help can come by sharing your feelings with a close friend or counsellor.

2 WHAT CAN I DO?

Although it may be very painful it will help if you can allow yourself to express what you feel. There is nothing to be ashamed about in giving vent to your feelings and it will help prevent greater difficulties in the future. Grief can get stored away inside if it is not let out. It is natural to grieve over such a loss. You are not being weak or silly if you cry. Do not feel you are letting down yourself or your loved one.

Why did it have to happen?

It is hard to find an answer. We wrestle with it, especially when the death was unexpected. When it happens to someone in the prime of life, or to a young person or child, it seems such a terrible waste. Although there may be reasons why it happened, an accident or illness, explanations do not really bring comfort at this point. It is a problem that goes much deeper. You may never discover a fully satisfactory answer but normally and gradually you will find you are able to live with it and to some extent come to terms with it.

My feelings surprise me

Bereavement is very upsetting. You may be frightened and bewildered by unexpected thoughts and strong feelings. There may be anger, against God, the doctor, other people, yourself or even the one who has died. You are hurt and afraid and it is natural to feel angry at everything that has caused such pain. When you lose something you search hard to recover it. This is the kind of feeling we have when someone important to us dies, but we cannot get our loved one back and this can cause frustration and anger.

You may have nursed the person who has died and now be upset at feeling relief that his or her suffering is over. At times tears come at even the slightest thing. At other times you will be dry-eyed and feel empty. It may seem all purpose has gone out of life and there is nothing left to do. If the death occurred in a hospital or hospice or care home you may be upset because you were not able to look after your loved one near the end of their life. There are likely to be moments when you feel very close to the one who has died. You may think you see or hear them near at hand and find you are actually talking out loud to him or her. This can be comforting but may also be a little frightening. At other times you may worry because you cannot recall how he or she looked, feeling you have lost touch forever. All this is normal, a natural part of coming to terms with what has happened.

I can't concentrate anymore

Everything is shaken up by your loss. You feel restless and unsettled. You cannot be bothered, things seem so trivial. You will probably find you make a decision and then do something else instead and it is not uncommon to forget what you are doing, even in the middle of simple tasks. It is hard to concentrate when your mind is so full of what has happened. You will slowly recover your composure and the ability to do things again.

When you lose someone important you often realise in a new way how much he or she meant to you. The one who has gone provided many of the things that gave meaning to life. He or she may have taken care of the practical and financial matters you are now faced with. Bereavement takes us into unfamiliar territory. Some things may seem so enormous that you feel you will never cope. Try not to be too ambitious. Take things slowly. Live one day at a time. You have the capacity to survive and to do more than you think. Self-confidence can be one of the things hardest hit. Take encouragement from tackling and succeeding with what could seem a small achievement to others but may be a massive one for you.

Bereavement after a violent death

There have always been dangers but in the modern world they seem more indiscriminate and sudden particularly when caused by criminal action or natural disaster. The person you have lost may have been killed in this way. You may have heard the news from a television report with distressing pictures of the scene, catching you completely unprepared. All kinds of thoughts and feelings will have welled up. Desperation that your loved one may have been involved, searching your mind to try and work out where he or she may have been at that moment, growing panic over what to do, how to get more information. Needing to know but not wanting the dreadful news you fear. You may have heard the news from people talking about it, even commenting to you about it without you knowing you may be personally affected. Someone may have telephoned, a relative or friend to see how you are or to break the news. The call could have come from a stranger, a police officer or government official or a journalist. As you took the call you may not have known the reason for it.

However the news reached you the shock it brought will have been intense. It may have numbed you, may have made you restless particularly as you waited for more information, possibly for hours or days. The news may have given you unexpected energy. You may have reacted by not believing your relative or friend was involved, holding on to the hope they were elsewhere, had changed their routine or travel plans, or that they were injured and not killed. Not knowing is a terrible experience and in some circumstances this can go on for a long time. Most people's reaction is to want to go to the scene of the tragedy. It may have happened overseas which brings the complications of travel and language and ways of doing things. When we lose something we want, we need to search for it. This need is magnified if it is a person who is missing. Even if we know they have died the urge to go may remain strong. If this is how your bereavement came you may have already been to the place where it happened. This is part of grief, a connecting with the one who has died, a deep need to know something of their final hours, and also a way of making sure no mistake has been made and that they are not still alive somewhere. All this can be more acute if the body has not been recovered. When this happens a part of grieving can remain uncompleted.

Grief brought about by violent death can leave many things to be dealt with. Anger at those who caused it, incomprehension at their callousness, revengeful feelings towards them. In our pain it is understandable we want to hit out at those who caused the hurt. You may have found yourself with the distressing thought of blaming the one who has died for being there. Why did they go to a risky part of the world? Or blaming yourself – why didn't I stop them or persuade them to go elsewhere? Or blaming their work or sport for taking them there. Grief hurts and you are wounded and in your agony you are searching for answers.

The one who has died may be your spouse or partner,

your child, your parent. You may be a sibling, grandparent or grandchild. He or she may have been a great friend or work colleague. There is a widening circle of grief following every death and when it is as a result of an event that is national and international news that circle is wider still. A neighbourhood, a community, a nation, feels the loss. You may find this wider expression of grief comforting, knowing that so many people care. But it may be hard too. So many reminders. So much discussion. So much expectation that you will attend public and religious events. You may have mixed feelings over all this, including appreciation that the loss is widely felt, but also concern that your own grief and that of those close to you does not get submerged.

You may have to cope with media coverage. There is likely to be interest in your personal story not just in the early days but later too – when more details are known about what happened and probably on its first anniversary. You may be prepared to give interviews and find it helpful to do so but you may feel that the interest is intrusive. It is hard to say 'no' to the media. If you do not want to talk to reporters try and be firm with your 'no' or get someone close to be firm for you.

Seeking compensation

If death is caused by neglect or deliberate action it can leave those bereaved with a difficult decision. Whether or not to press, legally or informally, for compensation. Much will depend on the circumstances and the outcome of any court case that might be brought. What is undoubtedly important is for you to take trustworthy and competent advice if you are considering taking action for compensation. If you have access to a solicitor that could be a starting point. If not you may find it helpful to contact one of the bereavement organisations listed at the end of the book or your local Citizens Advice Bureau.

Seeking compensation is more than a practical matter. Your feelings are going to be part of the decision. You may wish to take action to teach the organisation or individual a lesson. You may have understandable anger that you feel can only be diminished if those who caused the death suffer too. Money is the usual method of compensation and you may be concerned your motives could be misinterpreted. Somewhere in you may be the thought that those responsible for the death owe something, not to you so much as the one who has died. Sometimes those receiving compensation donate it to a charity.

Alongside the seeking of compensation can be the strong desire to ensure nothing similar happens again, maybe pressing for a change in the law, or a proper crossing on a busy road or change of practices in a workplace. This may be something you are engaged in or would like to do. Grieving can produce energy and commitment to a cause and lead to benefits for many people. It can be a way of channelling powerful feelings.

There are risks in pressing for compensation or taking up a cause. It can be exhausting and take a long time. You may have to be aware of exploitation by those who see gain in it for themselves. The media may well take an interest which can be a mixed blessing as it helps the promoting of your cause or case but it may entail intrusive and unhelpful reporting. There is the possibility you may have contact with the family and friends of those who caused the death through attendance at court or in some other way with all the emotions this may evoke. There is a risk that your claim may be denied.

The actions you take can be a positive focus for your grief, bring a sense of achievement and be a lasting memorial to the one who has died. But it may have meant some of your grieving has been set aside for a while and remains to be faced. Afterwards, you may feel a sense of anticlimax and a loss of purpose. If you are thinking of claiming compensation or taking up a cause you may find it helpful to share your thoughts with good friends and get sound advice and counselling help.

Bereavement after turning off a life support machine
You, along with the medical team, may have been faced with the dilemma of whether or when to switch off a life support machine. It may have seemed an impossible choice for which there is no right answer. You would not want to prolong any suffering nor maintain a life that was never going to be able to respond, but to be the one who decides about the life or death of someone you love is deeply agonising. You may have been able to take the decision or you may have left it to the doctors. Whichever way it was you will feel the anguish of the decision and need the love and understanding of those around you and possibly the availability of counselling help.

3 WHAT HAS TO BE DONE?

Letting people know

Close relatives and friends should be told of the death first, while others may be informed once the details of the funeral are known. If you feel unable to speak to anyone yourself ask someone close to do it for you. They can ask those they tell to pass the news on to others. An entry in a newspaper can be a way of letting a wider circle know. Those who should be told, some of them after the funeral, include:

children's school or college (as soon as possible)
employer and business contacts
your own employer
Department of Social Security
bank
tax office
insurance companies
executors of the will
Trade Union
organisations or clubs
solicitor
accountant
house landlord
providers of mortgages, loans, hire purchase
    agreements, standing orders, direct debits, credit
    cards
pension providers.

Registering the death

The doctor who looked after the one who has died, at home, in a hospital or hospice or care home, will give you a death certificate. If there is to be a cremation you may need two certificates, signed by different doctors. In England and Wales a death should be registered within five days. This is done at the Registry of Births, Deaths and Marriages in the area where the death happened. In Northern Ireland the registration should be as soon as possible but not later than five days. In Scotland the death should be registered within eight days. Whoever goes to the Registry Office will need to take the death certificate and personal documents relating to the one who has died such as birth and marriage certificates. If you cannot find the personal documents at the time the death can still be registered. There are some occasions when a death has to be reported to a Coroner. If this happens the Coroner will tell the Registrar when to issue the death certificate. In this case it is possible there may be a delay in arranging the funeral. Registry Office addresses are in the telephone book and if the death took place in a hospital or hospice the staff there will have the details. The addresses and other information can also be found on the Government websites.

It is likely you will need more than one copy of the registry certificate to claim benefits, life insurance and so on. The Registrar will provide the extra copies. In some cases there may be a charge for these.

Registering a death can be upsetting. If possible take someone with you. If you are not able to go yourself ask another member of the family to do it for you.

Flowers

People may wish to send flowers for the funeral. You may prefer family flowers only and if you wish you can suggest donations to a charity or organisation instead of flowers. What happens to the flowers after the funeral will depend on whether it was a cremation or burial. If a cremation the most personal ones usually remain with the coffin and the remainder will be placed where you can look at them after the service. They are normally left there for at least a day before removal. If it is a burial the flowers will be placed on top of the grave and left there for several days. If you wish you can ask that the flowers be given to a hospital or hospice after the funeral. The Funeral Director will be able to deal with this for you.

State benefits

It will be necessary to contact your local Social Security Office if social security benefits are being claimed. It may be possible for someone from there to come and see you. It will be helpful to have someone with you if you go to the office or an official visits you at home. The address will be in the telephone book or on the Social Security website. Leaflets in a number of languages, are available to help you discover what benefits you may be entitled to and how to claim. You can ask for them to be posted to you. Your local Citizens Advice Bureau will also have information as will the Social Security website.

A will

There may be a will. If so, its executor – the person appointed to make sure the instructions are carried out – will deal with it. It may be somewhere in the house or at a bank or with the solicitor who drew it up. The executor will need to be informed of the death. If no will has been made you may have to apply to the Probate Registry for what are called 'Letters of Administration'. There is some difference in the procedure depending on where you live. In Scotland it is called Grant of Confirmation, and application is made to the local Sheriff's Court.

In the absence of a will or any other form of clear instructions you may want to take your time deciding what to do with certain possessions, if you are responsible for them, and whether or not they should be given to other people. You may have to be involved in clearing a house after the death. This can be a sad experience evoking many memories and it may be a help to take your time over it and if there are other family members to talk together about things to be kept, distributed to family and friends or disposed of in other ways.

There are some things I'm not sure about
Knowing where to turn for help in bereavement can be hard enough and can be made worse if you do not know very much about the various helping agencies, both statutory and voluntary. You may not be familiar with filling in forms. You may have tried to get help in the past and been frustrated or confused by officials, or been passed from one agency to another, or given several telephone numbers to ring. Some of the leaflets on benefits and other kinds of help are not always easy to understand. All of this can seem overwhelming. If you need practical or financial help it is important you should receive it.

Someone in the family or a good friend may be able to help go through things with you. One of the organisations listed at the end may be a good starting point too. Do not worry if you feel unsure about what to say. They will help to explain things.

4 THE FUNERAL

You may be dreading the funeral. Some people remember their preparation for it and the funeral itself very clearly, but many go through it in a kind of haze. There can seem so much to think about and you may have mixed feelings about how much you want to be involved in the planning of the funeral or wishing someone would take the responsibility away. Afterwards you may find it helpful to ask someone close to you who was present to tell you about it.

A funeral is very important. It is part of saying goodbye, the ending of a chapter and the beginning of another. It is also a time for family, friends and colleagues to share in your sadness, show their support for you and express their own grief.

If you are having a religious service the people best able to help you with the arrangements are the church minister or other religious leader who will be conducting the funeral and the funeral director. They will be able to discuss with you when and where the funeral should be held, the kind of service you would like and whether it is to be a cremation or burial. You may not have arranged a funeral before and it is important you have all the information you need to help you make decisions, and to talk about it with others closely involved. This is particularly important if there are family members or friends who wish to take part formally in the service, paying a tribute or doing a reading, and over the decision where the body is to be buried or the ashes placed.

The funeral director will also be able to tell you how much the funeral will cost. Although you may not feel like discussing money at this stage it is important you get an estimate of how much you will have to pay. Even a simple funeral may cost more than you are expecting. It will help if someone can be with you when you discuss the arrangements so that they can ask questions you may not think of and make notes of the conversation for you. If you are unsure about the choice of funeral director or religious leader to conduct the funeral talk it over with the family or friends who may be able to offer suggestions.

If you do not wish to have a religious service there are alternatives and the funeral director will be able to advise you.

There may be special circumstances that will affect the funeral arrangements such as the non-recovery of the body or a death abroad or the donation of the body for medical research. If this is the case you will need advice and information on what to do and it may be necessary to talk to a solicitor, a doctor, the police or a government official. A funeral director can again be a useful source of advice. If it has not been possible to recover the body a service can still be held that includes some of the elements of a funeral. Whilst this may not enable you to deal fully with not having the body to lay to rest it usually brings some comfort.

As human beings we have a deep need to know the final resting place of our loved ones. If circumstances mean this is overseas you may be thinking of paying a visit to the grave or place where he or she died. You may not be able to do this for a variety of reasons and if this is the situation it may be possible for someone to take photographs for you.

Should I go and see the body?

If it is not against your religious or cultural practise going to see the body often helps and is another opportunity for 'saying goodbye'. It may be in a room at the funeral directors or in a hospice or hospital. You will probably find it comforting if someone comes with you. You may be advised by some not to see the body because they feel it will upset you too much. The important thing is that if you wish to do so you should be allowed to. If the children are old enough discuss with them if they would like to come with you.

In some circumstances you may be asked to identify a body as next of kin. This is likely to be very distressing. Make sure someone comes with you. If they do not come into the room with you it is important they are there to meet you afterwards and accompany you home.

Should I stick to the funeral plans we talked about?

The one who has died may have let it be known whether he or she wished to be buried or cremated. This may have been stated in a will. Usually this does not lead to any difficulties but you may feel you would like the arrangements to be different. It can be hard to choose between what your loved one wished and what you feel you need. Much will depend on the strength of the suggestions. If you feel you have made a promise you will probably wish to keep it. On the other hand if it was only a suggestion you may decide to be guided by what your feelings and thoughts are now. Like so many other things it will help if you are able to talk this over with someone.

If there is to be a cremation you will need at some point to decide what to do with the ashes. You may wish to have them scattered in the garden of remembrance at the crematorium or in a place of special meaning for you, or buried in a cemetery. You may want to have the person's name recorded in a book of remembrance or have a special plaque put up at the crematorium or cemetery. The funeral director will be able to provide you with information about what to do. If you are unsure take your time before deciding.

If there is to be a burial you may wish to have a head-stone placed on the grave. This usually takes place a few months after the funeral. For some people this stone lay-ing is an important ritual. If you are having a headstone it will be best to obtain a cost quotation first. This is something you can deal with later when you feel you are ready.

What about children going to the funeral?
If children wish to go they should be allowed to attend. They too are grieving and need the opportunity to share in the funeral with the adults. If they do not want to go pres-sure should not be put on them to do so. Much will depend on their age and how able they are to discuss things with you. If they wish to go it will help if someone can explain to them in advance what will happen. This will help them particularly at the point in the service when the coffin is either lowered into the ground or goes from view at the crematorium. You may find it helpful too to hear this explanation. It is possible this is the first funeral you have been to or the first of someone close.

It will be helpful for the children if someone they know well can stay close to them at the service and afterwards as well so they can be supported and comforted. If they do not go to the funeral make sure someone they know well is with them. It is best if they are not sent to school or excluded from the family and circle of friends, and if they have been elsewhere they should return home once everyone has come back from the funeral. Nothing should be done to make them feel left out.

What about the letters and people who call?
Letters and cards of sympathy are likely to arrive. You may feel you want to answer them personally or alternatively send a printed card of appreciation. Do this when you feel ready. People may telephone to see how you are and some will probably call to see you. Do not feel you have to do anything special to welcome them. Simply sitting quietly together or talking will help. Friends are sometimes unsure whether they should mention the one who has died by name, fearing they will upset you. You can take a lead by speaking of him or her yourself. You may find yourself crying but there is nothing weak or silly about tears at this time. They can be a positive help, a natural expression of the loss you feel.

It happened whilst I was away
Sometimes a death occurs when we are away, maybe overseas on holiday or business or living abroad. This can lead to the difficult decision over whether or not to return for the funeral. In some cases this will be a straightforward decision, in others far from easy. Those at home may have felt it best not to inform you until later. If you were told they may want to persuade you not to return for the funeral. If this has happened to you and you did not attend the funeral you may be feeling guilty about it. You may feel others will think less of you for not being there. These thoughts may persist and like other reactions are often best helped by sharing them with others.

Rituals
The first anniversary of the death and funeral may be

reached with mixed feelings – a sharpening of the sadness as you and others recall the past, and maybe too some sense of relief that the first year has passed, a year in which everything has had to be done for the first time without the one who has died. It will have been twelve months that included birthdays, Christmas and other special days and probably some important rituals such as a stone laying or the scattering or burying of ashes. There may have been other memorials. An entry in a book of remembrance, a memorial service, the placing of an inscribed seat or a tree planting.

Rituals, religious and social, are very important. Some of them may have been just for you and those close to you. Others might have involved a wider group, a school, an organisation, the armed services, the local community. One person's death may be mourned by many people. On these occasions you may have had the mixed feelings of sorrow and pride.

Rituals are not confined to the first year or to any period of time. You may find them comforting in the future too. Visits to a cemetery or crematorium garden, annual services of remembrance and thanksgiving, pilgrimages to special places, family gatherings on significant anniversaries, the giving of a gift of something belonging to the one who has died to a child or grandchild. Some rituals are provided by the church or other faith community or by a hospice and at them you will join others who are also bereaved. Follow your feelings as to how long you want to attend these events.

You may invent your own occasions, informal actions that hold meaning for you that you carry out alone. Rituals aid our remembering and mark a deep personal experience. They can be a means of helping us move on in our grief.

5 WHAT ABOUT MY HEALTH?

Nothing remains untouched by a major bereavement and you may be affected physically. You may lose your appetite, find it hard to get to sleep or have disturbed nights. Palpitations, heavy sighing and a feeling of needing to swallow often are not uncommon. You may experience tenseness, and aches and pains may be more common. Women may either miss or have irregular periods for a while. You may lack energy and motivation.

Grief can be very tiring. If you have been nursing the one who has died, maybe for a long time, you are likely to feel worn out and you will need time to regain your strength.

It is important to see your doctor if you are concerned about your own health or the health of others in the family. Ask for a thorough check-up and tell the doctor as much as you can about how you feel. Do not regard anything as unimportant and do not feel you have wasted the doctor's time if you are reassured there is nothing physically wrong.

The doctor may suggest medication. Do not hesitate to discuss this with him and ask what the medication is for, whether there may be side effects and when you should come and see him again. The doctor may choose not to prescribe anything because he feels that you will cope better without medication. Drugs may seem to bring relief but this is likely to be temporary and there is a risk that

31

dependence on them may delay the processes of grief and this could lead to greater problems later.

In grief you may not think as clearly or function as well as you normally do. Take care if you drive or handle machinery around the house or at work. Your concentration is likely to be affected for a while and the danger of accidents can increase. Give yourself time to settle and feel more confident before taking any risks.

Family doctors

Although your doctor should always be consulted if you are worried about your health a busy practise may not seem to allow sufficient time for the length of conversation you may feel you need. It will help when making the appointment to let the doctor or receptionist know that you would be grateful for a reasonable length of time to fully discuss how you are feeling. Some practises have counsellors available and it may be suggested you see one. We need to remember that, like the rest of us, doctors too may sometimes have difficulty talking about death or dealing with someone's grief.

6 KEEPING THE FAMILY TOGETHER

The person who has died will be missed by a lot of people. He or she may have been a spouse or partner, a parent, a grandparent, a child, a brother or sister, a close relative, a long standing friend, a trusted colleague. In our modern living it can mean an even wider circle – step-parents and grandparents, step-children and the extended step-family. Sometimes relationships are difficult and a death can add more complications. A funeral, the decision over whether burial or cremation, bequests from a will, are all painful enough and it is a time for sensitivity and tact and a thoughtfulness that tries to consider all who are closely involved. In the early days of grieving, and later too, this may be a difficult thing to do. When we are bereaved we have to make some of the most difficult decisions of our life at a time when we feel less able to and maybe without the one we shared decisions with in the past.

You may feel you are at the centre of all this and that the onus is on you to keep the family together. You may have young children or aging parents or others making demands on your time and energy. You may feel you have no choice but to put others first and your own needs on hold. This may come as a kind of relief as activity through the day and exhaustion at night leaves little space for your own thoughts and feelings. It is hard to keep the balance, attending to others, accepting help for yourself or declining it, being independent of others or allowing yourself some reliance on them. Your needs matter, your grief is important. There may seem no answer to this but try and find some time for yourself, allow those you trust to help out, and if you feel you need it seek personal support and practical help from outside the family and circle of friends. When we are low it is hard to seek help and there may be feelings of guilt but your recovery and your health are important for those you are caring for and for yourself.

Mingled families
Mingled families are increasingly common, step-relationships as a result of divorce and new partnerships. This may lead to some uncertainty and tension when there is a death. If relationships are good such things as attendance at the funeral, bequests from a will and keeping contact with former partners and family may not be a problem, but where they are strained it can add difficulties. In all that has to be done following a death emotions are tender and it is easy for things to be forgotten. It will be helpful both in the immediate days and later on if there can be good communication, allowances made for heightened feelings, with everyone as sensitive to each other as possible.

7 CHILDREN

A child shouldn't die

A baby's death is devastating. You may have had a still-birth and be surprised by the strength of your grief. There can be great distress too over a miscarriage. You may be upset because you feel other people do not seem to realise how much the loss has meant to you. You have been preparing for a baby but now there is no little one to love and care for. You may feel unable to come to terms with what has happened. You may be wrestling with questions – 'Did I do anything wrong?', 'Is it my fault?' You may wonder over possible future pregnancies. These are natural feelings when you lose a baby. You need comfort and understanding from those around you, as will your partner and any other children you may have. It is a time for sensitive support for all involved.

The child who has died may have been older. If the death was an accident or because of a sudden illness you are likely to have lots of questions in your mind, possibly with feelings of anger and guilt. If you have watched and nursed a sick child in hospital or hospice as the illness got worse, you may feel defeated and worn out. Everyone in the family needs support and you all need to care for each other. Do not hold back from seeking and accepting help. The place where your child was cared for will be able to offer support and there are the organisations listed at the end of this book.

If a baby or young child has died you may want to have another child fairly quickly. This can be a natural response to your loss but such a thought is best discussed fully before making a decision. It will help if the pain can be worked through as far as possible before trying for another child. You can never replace a lost child and should another baby be born it is important he or she be seen as a person in their own right and not as a substitute for the one who has died.

It is hard for a parent when their child dies before they do. It seems an overturning of what we see as the natural order of things. An elderly parent losing an adult child will often question why they have survived and not their son or daughter. Grandparents will often experience a double kind of bereavement. Their grief over the death of a grandchild and their sorrow for its parents.

Do children feel the loss?
Yes, very much at times. Everyone who has had affection for and close ties with the one who has died will be grieving in some way. The death of a parent, brother, sister or grandparent is an important loss for a child. He or she will have been part of his world, have looked after him, been his playmate, given him security and comforted him when he was upset. The one who has died will be greatly missed.

The age of the child may determine how he or she responds. Young children, who will not yet understand as much as older ones do about the finality of death, may appear not to be grieving. Nevertheless they have feelings and fears and these need opportunity for expression. Their secure world can feel threatened; they may be bewildered by what has happened and by the reactions of those around them. They will be aware even if only through sensing it that things have changed. Like you they may feel sad. A young child might not be able to put all these feelings into words although there could be questions which may be upsetting for you and hard to respond to. He or she may want you to be near them as much as possible and may be more upset than usual when you are not. There might be more irritability over trivial things.

The older child, understanding more of what is happening, will feel the loss keenly. He or she may be at an age when their own and other people's emotions are embarrassing and they may need help to know that tears and talking about their loss is all right. They may be feeling uncertain over the future and how the death will affect it. If it is possible to encourage them to share their thoughts and feelings it will help them and you to feel understood and supported. Any apparent indifference they seem to be showing may be a way of defending themselves from getting too upset. Do not feel hurt if they find it easier to talk to others about what has happened, maybe someone their own age or another member of the family.

Bereaved children do not always respond in ways adults think they might and the important thing to know is that children do grieve and that they need attention and support.

How can I help them?
You all need each other's love and care and sharing your sadness together can help. You may be worried over crying in front of them, and it can be frightening for a child if a parent seems to have completely lost control, but it is better if you and the children express feelings rather than bottle them up, and doing it together is comforting.

Try to answer their questions simply, briefly and honestly. It is so hard to have to tell children, even older ones, that someone they love has died. Try if possible to tell them yourself. If you feel this is too painful, be with them when they are told. Like adults their first reaction may be disbelief which is a combination of not being able to take it in and not wanting to accept it. They need time to absorb it. Try to avoid saying things like 'gone to sleep' or 'gone away' instead of using the words death or dead. They need to be helped to understand that death means the person is not coming back.

Some of their questions may seem inappropriate and trivial to an adult but can loom large in a child's mind. 'Who will cook our meals?' 'Can I still have my birthday party?' Underlying such questions may be a sense of insecurity with the changed situation. Quiet reassurance, along the lines of 'I will make sure that is taken care of', will help. Some questions may be deeper: 'Why did he have to die?' 'Where is she now?' If you have a personal faith this may determine your answer but care needs to be taken over trying to give a child an adult explanation, or one that might lead to confusion. Children can have imaginary ideas of what has happened and sometimes it is necessary to correct a misunderstanding. A straightforward answer, if it is true, may help: 'He was very sick and his body couldn't take anymore.' At times it may be sufficient to say 'I don't know but I'm here and we'll help each other.' There are a number of books for reading to young children which will help them. The organisations mentioned at the end will have suggestions. Try and let children know they can come back with other questions either at the time or later.

In the pain of the situation you may get on each other's nerves at times. Everyone in the family needs to try to make allowances and not put pressure on one another. This may be particularly true for an older child who may feel that he or she has to somehow replace the one who has died. Children may also feel that others expect them to undertake this responsibility.

It is important to keep the memory of the dead person alive for the children's sake. Gradually you will find you can talk more openly and refer to him or her in normal conversation. Photographs and personal things around the house will help you all to face the reality of the loss.

Try to be yourself with the children. If they see that you allow your grief to show they will feel more able to express their own. For the young child cuddles can be very comforting.

If it is a parent who has died it is possible a bereaved child may feel different to other children who still have their parents. It is best not to assume they will carry the news of the death to school. If you can do this yourself or ask someone close to do it. It is likely there will be others in the child's group of friends who may have lost a parent through death or whose parents are separated.

Sometimes children think they have caused the person to die by something they have or have not done or said. If they feel this way they will need reassurance this was not the case. If they are old enough to understand it can be explained to them that these are normal thoughts to have. This will help remove any sense of self-blame which might otherwise persist. If you are able to keep up as much of a routine as possible this will help children feel more secure. This may not be easy and you might want to think of enlisting the help of other people to look after such things as meals and other everyday matters for a while.

Young children are not able to sustain intense emotions for long and they may need permission to go off and play without feeling guilty.

8 A YOUNG PERSON'S GRIEF

Your bereavement may have come at a time when lots of other things are happening in your life, some of which may be unsettling. Perhaps you are changing schools or sitting important exams, or deciding between university or employment, or whether or not to have a gap year travelling. You may have started a new relationship or have had a break-up with a girl or boyfriend. You may want to see yourself as an adult and want others to treat you as one. You have your own life to live and want to make your own mind up about things.

The death of someone close may have come unexpectedly but even if you knew it was going to happen it would have been hard to anticipate its effect on those around you and on yourself. It can change everything. You may wish it had not happened, not only because you want the person to still be alive, but also because of the impact it has had and the major interruption it has brought to your life. You may be embarrassed by your feelings and by the crying and sadness of others. You may not want the school or college or work authorities to know about the death because you do not want to be singled out or have any special treatment. Yet it is important they do know so they can understand if your studies or concentration are affected. You may want your friends to keep off the subject and act as usual towards you, although you may find it easier to talk to them than anyone else. The chances are that your circle of friends includes those who have also had a serious loss, maybe through death or the separation of parents. Exchanging experiences can be helpful.

Things will have changed at home and this can be very unsettling. Family income may be reduced, plans may have to be cancelled and you may be having second thoughts over doing what you had wanted to do about your education or career. You may feel some responsibility to take care of things, to do something to help. You may sense others are wanting you to act this way, could even be saying so, and you might be resenting the pressure.

There may be times when you feel left out of things or that your grief has not been acknowledged. When we are young and grieving we want it recognized but we do not want a spotlight on it. We may feel we do not want too much sympathy or conversation about it. You may be part of a family where thoughts and feelings are shared and hurt expressed and where others are sensitive to your feelings. It may be your family finds these things more difficult.

You may have to decide when it is right for you to go back to your place of education or work after the death. And there may be other decisions – when to start having friends around again or going out to parties or entertainment. There are no hard and fast rules. Be guided by your feelings and talk to your family and friends. Try to accept how others are feeling and to help them see how you feel.

Bereavement can disrupt the life of an individual and family and it takes time before a new pattern emerges. It can be hard sometimes to respond to other people's needs and wishes and have yours met as well. A bereavement can also bind a family closer together and do the same for a group of friends. Though not always easy to share things with others it is important to talk together about the major issues and important decisions.

Grief can be very painful and you will deal with it in your own way as others do in theirs. Whatever age you are, help is available from outside the network of family and friends and some organisations offer particular support to young people. There is a list at the end of the book. If you feel at any time, not just in the early months but later too, that you are stuck with thoughts and feelings that will not change or go away think about getting help for yourself. It is not silly or cowardly to do this. Like a physical pain, the hurt of grief may be temporarily eased by alcohol or drugs, but they provide respite not recovery. Working through grief is hard and takes time and you will carry some experience of your loss into the future. Allowing yourself to express your emotions and thoughts with those you trust can be the most positive way of moving on.

As time goes by you may reach a particular anniversary of the death or a major point in your life when you want to do something special, either on your own or with others. If this happens, respond to your feelings and do what you feel important. It may be raising money for a charity or undertaking some challenge in memory of the one who has died. It is likely this will be another of the stages of healing.

As you grow older it is not unusual to feel a little anxious about your own health as you approach the age at which the person you have lost died. If this sets off a worry for you make sure you see your doctor.

9 BEING A MUM AND DAD

If it is your spouse or partner who has died and you have young children to look after you may have some anxiety about providing the all-round care they need. It may not be easy to find someone suitable to look after them while you are at work, especially at school holiday times, and it can be expensive. If you employ a childminder or put your child in a pre-school group or after school club it is important to check the individual or group are properly registered and that you happy with them. It will be re-assuring for you if you personally meet those who will have your child in their care. Talk with the children about what is happening, prepare them for changes and try to answer any questions they may have. It may be upsetting for you to have to leave your child in the care of someone else.

Possible sources of advice and information include the child's teacher, the health visitor, your doctor, the local social services department or one of the organisations listed later.

What about the children going back to school?
They will probably want to stay close to you for a while. They may be afraid you are going to die too. Discuss with them how they are feel about going back to school, or if they are older, to work or college.

10 SAME-SEX BEREAVEMENT

The person who has died may have been your partner in a homosexual or lesbian relationship. You may feel your loss is being acknowledged and your grief recognised and that there are people to turn to for support. But for some this can be a time of loneliness and isolation, particularly if the relationship was not known about or accepted by others. You may feel excluded, especially if you have not been involved in funeral arrangements or included in family events. You may find it helpful to contact the Gay Bereavement Project or one of the other organisations listed at the end.

11 DEATH OF AN IMPORTANT CARER

For some the death of a family member or close friend can mean additional loss. The person who has died may have been their carer and the reason they were able to live in the family home. There may be difficulties to do with mobility or sight, possibly with mental ill-health or comprehension and communication. The death may mean a move into residential care, giving up the home and leaving familiar things, places and people. We all grieve in our own way and we all need help of some kind in bereavement. The apparent inability to articulate grief does not mean loss is not felt. If the death of a carer leads to leaving the family home it is a double kind of loss. If this has happened to you, or someone close to you, try to share feelings and fears and get specialist help if needed.

12 SUICIDE

I did not expect it to happen this way

Some people take their own lives and the grief following a suicide is hard to deal with. Especially difficult are the feelings of rejection and guilt. There may be anger too that you have been left to deal with the aftermath of a suicide, maybe on your own. You may be reluctant at first to tell others how the death happened, but if you are able to share it you are likely to feel a sense of relief that you have done so. It will also help others to understand more of what you are going through. You may find it helpful to talk first to a close friend, your doctor or someone from one of the bereavement organisations who will keep it confidential, and in a way enable you to rehearse what you might say to other people. This may be particularly helpful if you have children to tell.

You may have been the one who found the body. The shock would have been intense and the memory and images are likely to stay with you, possibly all your life. You will probably have had to tell the police but it may be too hard to talk about it with anyone else, especially those close to the one who has died and to you. If you can share things it will bring some relief and contacting one of the organisations listed at the end could be the starting point. You may have to attend and give evidence at an inquest which can cause distress. If you have to do this make sure you have someone close to you to go with you.

13 DECISIONS AND CHANGES

This is a time when you may be very vulnerable. Watch out for anyone who might try to take advantage of this. Take time over decisions that have to be made, and get all the advice you can until you are clear in your mind what needs doing and what the results of your actions will be. Try not to rush into things.

What are the things I should really think about?

If you have young children you may wish to consider guardianship for them in the event of your death. If you have not already done so you may need to think of making a will or bringing an existing one up to date. It may be important to check how you stand financially, open or change a bank account, check any credit or loan agreements, or transfer the house ownership or tenancy to your name. It is important you have sound advice if you are unsure what to do.

There may be a number of things to return. Passport, pension book, driving licence, season tickets, membership cards, car or other insurance documents. On these and other things there may be a refund for unused portions.

If there are any worrying unpaid bills either write, or ask someone to write for you, and explain what has happened, asking for time to sort things out. Take your time over any decisions involving money. Do not throw away financial documents until you are clear they are no longer needed.

Citizens Advice Bureau will be able to advise
how long this may be. Keep a copy of any official
le. you write as it may be helpful and important to
know what you said at the time.

Coping with change

Bereavement brings changes. In the early days of grief if
you are now on your own you may have to wrestle with the
decision of going away to a family member or friend for a
while or staying at home. You may be torn over what to do.
You may feel under pressure to respond to an invitation to
stay with someone for a few days. It can be comforting
to be with others and be looked after, but you may be concerned about having to return to an empty house or not
wanting to become a burden to them. The decision may be
over an offer from someone to come and stay with you for
a time. This may be easier to accept, bringing companionship without having to worry about coming back after
being away. Like all important decisions it will help if you
can talk these things through with family or friends so that
you can share what you are feeling. Hearing yourself
express uncertainties and concerns can help you become
clearer in your mind over what you want to do.

You are likely to adjust very slowly to not having the one
who has died around in the home anymore: choosing what
to eat, laying mealtime places, bedtime routines, television
viewing, school runs. Not having to take account of their
presence and needs is a major change.

If you have been caring for someone who has not been
well you may feel some relief that the responsibility has
ended, but with that can come some guilt that you feel this
way. You may also be faced with a new freedom, especially
if you have been caring for them for a long time, or have
been organising your days around hospital or hospice

visiting. As with most things in early grieving, give yourself time to adapt to the changed situation.

There are likely to be other changes too. When to return to work, when to resume social life, or return to Church or group for the first time. When to become a host or hostess again and invite people for dinner or coffee. What to do about a holiday: to go with others or on your own or not at all. And where to go. A known place with its comforting yet painful memories, or somewhere new with its adventure and uncertainties. If you have young children, there is the question of what to do in school holidays and how to balance family time and work commitments. Taking decisions in the unfamiliar situation that is bereavement is hard and lonely. Talk to those you trust to be sensitive and patient, listen to your own instincts, share what you are thinking with those involved and get sound advice. If something does not feel right for you and others, defer the decision if possible. Adjustment takes time and effort and makes demands on you. Wherever possible give yourself time and allow your inner resources to build. You may feel your ability to make decisions and your confidence to act is not coming back. In your gradual adjustment and recovery they will.

It is likely that some decisions cannot be avoided. They may be to do with money or where to live. You may have to do something about your own health which you have postponed until now. It may be an issue to do with the children or an elderly relative. If it is possible to ask for more time before resolving these issues you may want to do that. If you or someone on your behalf explains the situation to any official body that may be involved it is more likely to respond with some understanding. If a decision has to be made make sure you have all the information you need, talk it over with those involved, and if doubts remain when you have decided, try to reassure yourself you have done your best. Hard though it is, try to move on. Part of recovery in grief is eventually to allow the past to rest, to lay it down, and allow the present to exist and the future to be possible.

Should I move house?

Coming to terms with memories and familiar things around the house can be a very painful experience. It is tempting to think a move might help. You may feel under pressure to do so: the family may be encouraging you to think about it, to move nearer them. Maybe the house or garden seems too big. It is best to wait until you have properly thought through such a big decision.

If you are living in a tied house you may have to move. You are usually allowed time to make alternative arrangements. If you are uncertain over what will happen get all the information you can about what is involved.

What about personal possessions?

It may be difficult to decide when to go through the possessions of the one who has died and what to do with them. It can mean sorting through clothes, jewellery, tools and papers, and if it is a child who has died – through their playthings. Allow yourself plenty of time when you decide to do this. It will take longer than expected. It may at times be painful as you come across things that have special memory and meaning. You may want to ask someone to be with you as you go through things, or you may feel this is something you want to do on your own.

You may be under pressure to clear the house fairly quickly because it is to be sold. If you are not sure what to do with some items try to find a way of keeping them until you are ready to decide.

What about my work?

If you work take as much time off as you feel you need in consultation with your employer. If you think the formal allowance is not sufficient ask someone from the personnel department to discuss it with you.

If you have not been employed you may feel it is necessary to get a job for financial reasons. If no opportunities are immediately obvious you may wish to think about what you would most like to do, the skills and experience you already have and the possibility of training in new skills. It may not be financial need but personal fulfilment that leads you to think of employment.

14 TRYING TO COPE

The family

Everyone in a family is affected by the death of one of its members. At times it may seem you are not much help to each other. Conversations and silences can be equally upsetting and tensions can be high. You may be part of a family where relationships have not been good in the past and the death seems to have made things worse.

You may be concerned for others in the family and want to get them some help but be uncertain how to do so. It is possible they may reject it anyway. If possible encourage them to seek the help themselves. If this is how things are do not neglect to seek help for yourself. You can discuss in confidence your worries about others; this will be a help in itself and may open up ways for them to be offered support as well.

Families may be separated by distance, adding to the feelings of isolation. Where this is the case try to keep in regular touch through telephone, letters and emails. This is particularly important on anniversaries and special occasions especially if families cannot be together. Grandparents whose son or daughter has died may fear they will not see their grandchildren as often and this can be a cause of some tension. It calls for a lot of understanding to retain the family links, something that is very important for the children.

Abnormal grief

This book does not aim to address the needs of those who experience abnormal grief reactions, for whom psychiatric care may be appropriate. It is important that such help is sought as soon as possible. If you are concerned about a member of the family or a close friend who seems stuck in their grief, maybe with a prolonged deep depression, try to encourage them to see their doctor, or offer to make an appointment for them and go with them.

Bereaved in a care home

Your bereavement may have come whilst you are a resident in a retirement or nursing home and one of your friends there has died. It may be they were ill and had to go into hospital and you have not seen them again, or they were nursed in the home and you did not meet them at meal times or in the communal activities as you usually did. This may mean you did not have the chance to say good-bye. This could be distressing for you as close bonds are often built up in residential homes. This is likely to be more painful if you did not know of their declining health. Your sadness may also include thoughts about your own health and future. Try to share your feelings and thoughts and memories of the one who has died with staff and those who visit you.

Regrets

Regrets seem inevitable in bereavement. They are likely to be stronger if the death was sudden with no time for preparation. Even seemingly trivial things can be magnified into worries. Things done or not done, words spoken or left unsaid, can go round and round in your mind and you agonise over the 'if only'. It is so hard to accept that some things cannot be changed. You may blame yourself for being outspoken or thoughtless and it can be an almost overwhelming feeling. You may be angry with the one who has died that he or she did not help matters and that you are now left to carry this on your own. There are times in grief when emotions and thoughts can be in turmoil. Allow yourself to know these are normal feelings and that gradually things will calm.

If your regrets are over what was said to someone in the family or a friend wait until you are ready and talk to them about it.

If the regrets or guilty feelings persist you may find it helpful to talk about them to a good friend or a counsellor.

People expect me to grieve but I can't

There may be several reasons for this. It can take quite a while for the shock and numbness to recede. You may still find it hard, if not impossible, to accept that the death has happened. If the body has not been recovered, or you are clinging to the belief the person has not died, this can make acceptance and allowing yourself to grieve more difficult.

You may be so concerned to keep going for the sake of others that you have not yet allowed yourself to begin grieving. Or you may be feeling sadness when you are on your own but keeping it from others.

Sometimes we do not grieve in an expected way because there is little grief to express. The relationship may have been a poor one and the feelings now are of relief and freedom. This may lead to mixed-up emotions that can bring inner conflict. This does not mean you are not feeling some sense of loss. You may be trying to cope with some guilt over the way things were in the relationship and possibly feel under pressure to respond in the way others expect. It is hard to share this honestly as it can appear heartless and disloyal. Try to accept that this is how it is for you and if you continue to be troubled by it do seek help.

I am not looking forward to Christmas and holidays

Special times and anniversaries can be very painful. Once you have survived them you will feel stronger and more able to cope. Other people may be uncertain how to respond. Some will feel they should not intrude, others will want to give you support. It is comforting if others can acknowledge the importance of special days.

It can be especially painful to think about and take part in events the one who has died would have attended. You may have mixed feelings about going yourself whilst others will want you there but might be concerned over how upset you may be. If possible talk about it beforehand both to share your feelings, and in a way, to prepare yourself for it.

Is it morbid to visit the crematorium or grave?

Visiting the grave, or the place where ashes may have been scattered or buried, may be important to you. We often need a focus for grief, especially in the early days, and it will be an opportunity to take flowers and maintain the grave or memorial plaque. Others close to the one who has died may wish to visit too. If there are children who come too you may have to be prepared for questions and it provides a quiet opportunity for memories to be shared. Gradually you may feel you do not need to go quite so often. As time goes by if you feel much more upset than you expected over missing a visit it may be helpful to talk this over with someone.

If you live away from the area of the grave or ashes resting place and find it difficult to visit you may want to think of asking someone who would be willing to take flowers occasionally and particularly at special times.

There may be a part of the house where you keep special things associated with the one who has died on view. This can be comforting but if you begin to worry about relying on it too much again it may be helpful to talk to someone about it.

Will reading help?

Words seem so inadequate when you try to describe how you feel, none are expressive enough. The same is often true when others try to show their sympathy or offer words of comfort. Yet in grief words are very important. Those close to you want to show they care, in conversation, through letters and cards. Funeral and memorial services are built on words, and grave headstones and memorial plaques contain inscriptions that are often thought about long and hard as the right words are sought.

The written word can be helpful. Passages of scripture, poetry, a favourite hymn or song, someone's prayer or part of a familiar book can be comforting. What other bereaved people have written may have special meaning for you. Because every person's grief is so personal it is difficult to suggest some books rather than others. The organisations listed will have a wide range of leaflets and longer reading, for adults and children. There are a number of books for reading to younger children who are bereaved or for children to read themselves.

You may want to write something yourself, put down your experience, or keep a kind of diary. It is one of the ways of expressing your grief and many people have found it helpful. It is not necessarily for others to read, but it may be. It is essentially for you.

Help from the Internet

The Internet can be a useful source of information. The organisations listed later have their own websites, often with links to other resources, including helpful reading. Great care needs to be exercised when using the Internet especially if personal details or payment is requested. It is best to only become involved with such sites if you are absolutely sure of their security and genuineness. If you have any doubts do not make use of them or take sound advice before you do.

I have my faith

Having a religious faith will not necessarily reduce the pain of loss nor does it remove the importance of working through your grief. It does not mean you will not wrestle with questions, especially if the death was untimely. It can however be a great comfort and strength and, depending on your view, give some meaning to what happens after death. You want the one who has died to still be with you, but if that cannot be to believe their spirit or soul is now at peace for ever is a source of comfort and hope. You will find strength too if you believe in reunion after death.

Having faith usually means you belong to a community of caring people, in a church, synagogue, mosque or temple, and this can be a source not only of emotional and spiritual support but social and practical help as well. Belonging to such a ready-made group where you are already known can be a great help as you ease your way into community and social life again. It should also mean you have access to a spiritual and religious leader. Do not hesitate to ask them to call and see you.

I seem to have lost my faith

Religious faith can be shaken by bereavement. Suffering and death raise deep questions. 'Why me?' 'Why did it have to happen?' 'Why someone so young?' These are understandable but often there is no straightforward answer. Try not to feel too ashamed or inadequate to discuss things with your minister, rabbi, priest or religious leader. The Bible and other religious texts record many instances of anguish and searching. There is nothing wrong with honest doubt and questioning. If you feel your faith is weak you may find it comforting to lean on that of others for a while.

I have never had a religious faith

For some this is a matter of personal conviction, for others the existence of organised religion or the concept of a personal faith may not seem helpful or relevant in their lives. Others will freely admit they wish they had a faith and may envy those who do especially in times of need, but would find it dishonest to pretend belief that is not true for them. If this is where you stand you will have accepted that the pain of your bereavement will not be eased by the support of faith and you will be drawing on other inner resources. Whether or not you have a faith does not diminish the need for help from others, and receiving help from the organisations listed at the end does not depend on your view of religion. If you feel you would like to discuss issues of religion one starting point could be a conversation with a friend who has a faith.

Funerals do not have to have religious content and the British Humanist Society will have details of alternative funerals, as will a funeral director.

58

Bereavement rituals

Religious and cultural background and tradition play a part in how we cope in bereavement. You may have special and set rituals to perform at the time of the death, the burial or cremation may have to take place fairly quickly and there may be customs to be followed in the early months and when the first or other significant anniversaries come. You may also have a set period of mourning along with traditional family practices. It is important that these are performed properly for your peace of mind and to help your coping and recovery. If you need help, contact your religious leader, an older member of the family or the person best able to give advice within your community. There are organisations within cultural communities for those who are bereaved. If you have difficulty contacting them one of the organisations listed later will probably have details.

15 I CAN'T SEEM TO GET MOVING

When someone close to you dies it is as if a part of you has died as well. There are times in bereavement when you feel very low. You are carrying a heavy weight of loss and it is hard to take any interest in life, in others and even in yourself. At such times things may appear hopeless. If the feeling of being stuck continues it is important to seek help. Take heart that no mood lasts for ever.

I can't go on alone

So much has been bound up in the relationship, over many years or for a shorter time, that there can seem no point in going on. The years ahead may seem endless and without meaning. In the early days you may long to be with the one who has died and see your own death as a means of reunion. All this is a normal reaction to the emptiness of your life as you see it at the time.

There is however a lot of difference between feeling life is not worth living and actually thinking of suicide yourself. When you are very low hang on to the fact that the feeling will lift, however unlikely this may seem. Remember you are important to other people. If it helps make use of things that bring some comfort and reassurance such as poetry, a religious passage, music, certain possessions, sharing things with a friend. If you are worried by persistent thoughts of suicide it is very important to seek someone to talk to. A call to The Samaritans at any time of day or night will always get a response. Their number will be in the telephone book or the operator is usually able to put you through.

Your doctor or someone else in health care or one of the bereavement organisations are also sources of help.

Try to keep up a normal routine as much as possible. Do not overcrowd your life for you need time to grieve. Look after yourself and try not to let things slip out of control. Keep in contact with other people.

Pointers for coping

Every grief is uniquely personal. Only you had the relationship you had with the one who has died. Others had their unique relationship and will be grieving in their personal way too. Because it is so individual it cannot be planned for nor will it follow a straightforward pattern. It cannot be programmed to go in a certain way. However, there is some predictability to grief and some common ground with others who are bereaved, and it is important to know that what you feel and what you are going through are normal and natural. There can be comfort in this and in knowing others feel similar things to you.

You may also have within you something valuable that will help you cope now. Your own earlier experiences of loss and how you coped with them then. You may have gone through something that at the time you thought you would never deal with and survive but you did. It may have been the loss of a very prized possession or a missed opportunity, a major negative change in circumstances, the break-up of a relationship or the death of someone close. Losing is part of living and coping and coming through can

61

give you something to draw on in your grieving now. It may not seem much at present but be encouraged if you have survived loss before.

It is hard to see others enjoying themselves
You may wonder how the world can possibly go on. The happiness and companionship others have is in stark contrast to your own situation. It seems that no one is interested in you any more. It is as if others occupy their own world and you are outside it. Other people's reactions to you, which are often caused by embarrassment on their part, can be upsetting. Many people find the subject of death difficult to deal with and talk about and fear they will say the wrong thing. Because of this they may avoid the issue. Some, with the best of intentions, may try to offer you reassurance, for instance that the one who has died is no longer in pain or that, in a religious sense, they have gone to a better place. These may be thoughts that will bring reassurance later but at the time, especially if said not long after the death, can feel insensitive. Others may expect you to get over your loss quickly. This again may be because they are embarrassed or they are finding it painful to see your distress. One of the hardest things to cope with can be not getting invitations any more to couple-based occasions, or being asked so that you might be paired with someone else who is on their own.

All of this can make you feel isolated and hurt. Try not to let it lead to feelings of bitterness or to you cutting off contact with people.

I can't stand the loneliness
Loneliness is one of the hardest things in bereavement. Family and friends can help but it is something you have to come to grips with yourself. It takes a lot of courage to

walk into a new social situation but it becomes less frightening once you have done it. Self-confidence is hard hit. Your nerve may fail at the last minute. Try again.

Maintain contact with friends. If you are not up to visiting someone or responding to an invitation keep in touch by telephone or emails or letters. Let people know you want them to keep in touch with you.

There will be times when you prefer not to have people around you and other times when you long for them to be there. You may worry they will lose interest in you if you talk about yourself and what has happened too much. It can help if you express this concern and let them know how comforting it is to be with them. If someone offers to help or calls to see you and you do not feel up to it let them know you really appreciate their kindness and that you will be grateful if they could keep in touch and call again.

Painful reminders

Painful reminders are everywhere. A routine task shared before with the one who has died can feel empty and mechanical, a familiar place can be a 'no-go' area. Something you have planned and looked forward to seems pointless now, and you may have to make the difficult decision whether to go through with it or not. You can anticipate some reminders such as a special day, though it may not make it any easier to cope with, but on other occasions you are ambushed by events or words. A letter addressed to the one who has died arrives or someone telephones and asks for him or her. An official form requires filling in and you may be unsure how to deal with it. It is not always the bigger issues that bring the most pain or worry. Reminders of things shared just between the two of you can bring a deep sense of loss.

Some reminders are visual. You may be able to look at a still photograph but find it hard to watch the person who has died moving on film or hearing their recorded voice. Yet there can be comfort in this too. These recorded reminders are very important for children and for future generations as they learn about the one who is no longer here. Saying 'we have lost someone' when they have died is a true expression of how we feel, we are lost without them. But in a barely graspable way they are always with us and keeping their memory alive for yourself and others is important. There may be a place of special significance, a previous home or a venue where an important event took place that you want to introduce to your children or grand-children so that they can have a link with the past. Recollections, photographs, scrapbooks and other reminders are painful in our grieving and vital for our remembering.

The death of a famous person can reawaken our own grief. Hearing people's comments, seeing funeral services, reading obituaries, and getting caught up in public mourn-ing, can all come as a reminder of your own loss. So too does the death of someone else close to you, in the family or among friends. This may have happened whilst your own bereavement is recent and your grief raw and you may have relived all you have gone through.

Such reminders cause pain but for some they can also be helpful. It may be that for some reason you have not been able to express your grief, to let go and cry or speak about the one who had died. The death of someone else, or maybe of a pet, can be a kind of second chance and pro-vide a means of release for feelings that have been held back.

16 MEETING OTHER BEREAVED PEOPLE

You may want to meet others who have experienced bereavement. Although no two bereavements are ever the same, because each of us grieves what we have uniquely lost, this contact can be comforting and supportive. The organisations listed may be able to link you with other bereaved people. They may seem further on the road to recovery than you are but do not be discouraged. They will probably tell you they too were once in a similar position and that they are struggling still with some part of their own grief.

One way that many people have found to be a help, when they felt up to it, has been to do something on a regular basis for others in need. When you are ready to help others the experience you have had will be a valuable way of understanding what they are going through.

Help in a group

Some of the organisations listed at the end run support and counselling groups for bereaved people and there may be one in your area. They are usually led by a qualified person. Some are for those recently bereaved, others for parents or family groups, and some have groups for children. They have the aim of providing a safe place for the sharing of feelings and a stepping stone towards recovery. Additionally a local organisation might run such a group.

If you feel it would be helpful to go, at least once to try it out, your local Citizens Advice Bureau, doctor's surgery, community centre, church or telephone directory will have details. There may also be social groups for bereaved people locally. If so these can provide a valuable opportunity to regain some of your self-confidence in social things and be a means of making new friends.

Hospice bereavement care

If the one who has died has been cared for in a hospice you will probably have been given information about its bereavement care. This may include individual counselling and group support and possibly an invitation to return to the hospice for an act of remembrance after a few months. You may wonder if you are up to going on your own but you can usually take someone with you. It is another of the milestones on the journey of grief.

I have no one to turn to

For some 'being alone' means just that. They have no family, few if any friends. A widow or widower of a childless marriage, a single person who may have devoted much of life to caring for a parent, a shy teenager, an orphan, all may feel completely on their own. It is not always easy to find friends, make your way in a social group or pluck up the courage to seek help. One starting point can be to accept that there are others in a similar position. Contacting a bereavement organisation could be the beginning not only of sharing your grief but also of finding new links and making new friends.

17 DO I NEED HELP?

In your early grief you may not know what you need. People may offer their help or invite you to call them if you need them but it can be very difficult to decide, even to think about what to ask for. When the heartache and pain are deep and hard to bear, the loneliness constant, nothing seems to bring relief. In the early days it may feel it will always be like this. Looking ahead is impossible and the well meaning words of others as they try to reassure you things will get better can seem so untrue and may make you angry. Only after some time are you likely to even think of seeking help and the question may be how do I know if I need it?

You may find it useful, when you feel up to it, to ask the following questions of yourself. A kind of personal checklist.

- Do I feel I am coping with all that is happening and that I have enough inner resources, personal faith and strength of character to find my way through? Or do I feel I am struggling a lot with my emotions, blocking up my own crying, or finding it too painful to let others cry or talk about their feelings when they are with me? Am I trying to be busy all the time and avoiding quiet moments? Am I still finding it hard to accept the death has happened?
- Do I have family and friends who will be patient with me in my down as well as better moods, who will not

try to hurry my grief, who are on hand with practical help? People who will let me cry or talk or be dry-eyed and silent? Or do I feel no one understands how things are for me or that others are too busy with their own lives?

- Do I belong to a group, an organisation, that will be supportive? A Church or other Faith community, a self-help group, a social group of people my own age. Or do I feel I have no motivation to do things or go anywhere?
- Do I find it hard to be out of the house and, if I am, want to get back as soon as possible? Maybe I find it difficult to be at home and try to be out as much as possible. Do I feel I should not have to turn to others for help?
- Do I feel I need help but am not sure what will help or if anything can? Are particular things worrying me such as concern for others in the family, persistent guilt feelings, distressing images and memories that I am not able to be free of, not grieving as I or others think I should, how will I cope with a special date or occasion that is coming, or other worries?
- How do I find out what help is available?
- Should I contact one of the organisations for bereaved people? Will it be helpful if I saw a counsellor? Would I like to meet others who are bereaved?
- Do I need to see my doctor to talk about my health or poor sleep or symptoms that are worrying me?

How you answer these questions may be a guide to what kind of help you need. It may be helpful to go through them with someone whose wisdom and sensitivity you trust. If the questions prompt the thought of getting help a good starting point will be to contact one of the organisations listed later. You may find you will respond in a different way a few months later and whilst you may feel you would welcome one kind of support now it may be something else in a year's time. Though the pain may seem unending, grief is not a static thing and no mood is permanent. It may be hardly noticeable for some time but the ability to come through lies within you.

It can also help to have a kind of physical checklist.

- How am I sleeping?
- Am I eating enough?
- Am I smoking or drinking alcohol more than before?
- Do I mind how the house looks?
- Am I concentrating when I am at work or driving?
- Have I lost interest in things I used to be keen on?
- Am I aware of the needs of the family?

If any of these things are causing you to worry it could be an indication an appointment with your doctor would be helpful.

If you are unwell it is not uncommon in bereavement to think you may have symptoms similar to those experienced by the one who has died. This may not be the case but if you are worried and have questions arrange to see your doctor.

Asking for help

Some people find it hard to talk about personal issues and feelings with others but if you can possibly do so it will help. You may feel your loss is something you have to deal with on your own. In some ways this is true but do not let it stop you seeking support and advice from others. You may think that a particular problem is too trivial to interest others, but talking about it often helps prevent it getting out of proportion. It may be the case that talking to someone outside the family and friendship circles is easier. You may feel you do not want to become a burden to others or become over dependent on them. It is a matter of finding the balance between letting others help and doing things yourself.

It is hard because I am a professional carer
If you are in a helping profession you may find it difficult to grieve. This may be because you feel you should 'keep up' for the sake of others, or because of an image of yourself, or because of what others expect of you. Until now you will have been the one who provided counsel and support for others, the calm one in a crisis. But when the loss is personal, your loss, the grief your grief, you need to be allowed, and very importantly, to allow yourself to be a bereaved person. Otherwise there is a risk grief will be postponed and possibly make for greater difficulties later. As a professional you may feel you should be able to cope and not have to seek help for yourself, but it can be as important for you as anyone else. Your ability to help other people in their grief may well depend on how you respond to your own bereavement.

Adult: **€2.50**
Website: http://shelters.mellieha.info
Address: c/o World War II Mellieha Shelters,
Our Lady of Grotto Street, Mellieha, Malta

VAT NO: MT12973229

Nº 58182

18 WHAT ABOUT A NEW RELATIONSHIP?

Bereavement leaves you vulnerable, especially at a time when you need love, warmth and to feel personally cared for. If you have any doubts about a new relationship it may be best to hold back until you are clearer about things. If the other person is genuine he or she will respect your feelings. Loneliness, the yearning for companionship and sexual needs may all prompt the thought of a new relationship on a permanent basis. This is obviously a major step and you may want to give yourself time to work through your loss before moving into another deep partnership. Some people hurt by grief feel it is safer not to let themselves fall in love again. Some may see it as a moral duty to the one who has died to remain alone. Such thoughts are understandable for we can never replicate the relationship experienced with the one who has died nor replace a loved one. This does not mean however that a new relationship will not prove rewarding nor that it diminishes your love and memories for the one you are grieving. Contemplating a new relationship has ramifications for others, particularly children, including grown-up ones, and sensitive thought needs to be given to their reaction and to the timing of when they are told about the new person and when they might be introduced to each other.

How am I going to react sexually?
Sex may be something you are not interested in at first, but you may be surprised later by the strength of your sexual feelings. Some cope by pushing aside strong needs through will power, others engage in activities to channel their energies. Some may seek the self-relief of masturbation, others find their solution in reasoning things out and accepting this is something they have to live with. Casual relationships are rarely the answer. If you are worried about your sexual feelings do not hesitate to talk about it with your doctor, or someone experienced in sexual counselling, or contact one of the bereavement organisations.

19 CHERISHING YOURSELF

Often the best person to look after you is yourself. In the early days of grief this may be the last thing you think of. You may feel you cannot be bothered with cooking, especially if it is just for you, or with proper nourishment or your health care. Keeping in touch with others or making any future plans may seem too much of a burden and pointless. Gradually this will change and you will begin to take more of an interest in the world around you and in yourself. This is one of the signs of recovery, of the life force in you gently asserting itself. Looking after yourself, cherishing yourself, are very important. Make sure you eat regularly, sleep long enough, take some exercise, and keep up to date with any medication you are meant to take. When you feel able, invite friends for coffee or a meal and take up their invitations back. Treat yourself from time to time and on special days think of buying yourself a gift you would like in memory of the one who had died. Although there may be sadness in this there will hopefully be some pleasure too. Accept the moments of enjoyment that come and be kind to yourself over any tinge of guilt that may accompany them.

20 COMING THROUGH

Be patient with yourself. Take care of yourself. Give yourself time. Seek all the help and advice you need. Do not be frightened by the strength of feelings at times. Your recovery will not be in a straight line and there will be good and bad days. Bereavement is about remembering not forgetting. There will be times when you feel ambushed by memories or emotions. But if you do not try to avoid such things you will slowly feel stronger and more able to face the world again. Things that were hard to take earlier will become more acceptable later. You will begin to take more interest in yourself and in life generally.

In the midst of the heartache and in a way so hard to understand or accept, grief is a positive thing. It is a natural way of helping us cope with severe loss and the means by which we find recovery. In the early days you may find it hard to think that any meaning will return to your life. Allow yourself to believe it will.

21 ORGANISATIONS THAT CAN HELP

The following organisations offer help that covers the United Kingdom and some have a network of local branches or contacts. In addition there are a number of locally based organisations. Your local Citizens Advice Bureau or telephone book will have details.

Cruse-Bereavement Care offers help to all bereaved people by providing counselling, advice and information and opportunities for social contact.
Helpline telephone: 0870 167 1677
Young persons helpline: 0808 808 1677
Address: 126 Sheen Road, Richmond, Surrey TW9 1UR
Internet: www.crusebereavementcare.org.uk

Society of Compassionate Friends is an organisation of bereaved parents offering support to other bereaved parents.
Helpline: 0845 123 23 04
Address: 53 North Street, Bristol BS3 1EN
Internet: www.tcf.org.uk

Stillbirth and Neonatal Death Society offers support to parents and families bereaved by a stillbirth.
Helpline: 020 7436 5881
Address: 28 Portland Place, London W1B 1LY
Internet: www.uk-sands.org

Foundation for the Study of Infant Deaths supports families where a baby has died suddenly and unexpectedly.
Helpline: 0870 787 0554
Address: Artillery House, 11–19 Artillery Row, London SW1P 1RT
Internet: www.sids.org.uk

Winston's Wish offers support for children and young people up to eighteen and for parents and carers.
Helpline: 0845 203 0405
Internet: www.winstonswish.org.uk

National Association of Widows offers friendship and self-help to women whose husband or partner had died.
Telephone: 0845 838 2261
Address: 3rd Floor, 48 Queen's Road, Coventry CV1 3EH
Internet: www.nawidows.org.uk

Survivors of Bereavement by Suicide offers help to those bereaved by a suicide.
Helpline: 0870 241 3337
Address: Volserve House, 14–18 West Bar Green, Sheffield S1 2DA
Internet: www.sobs.admin.care4free.net

Lesbian and Gay Bereavement Project offers support and advice.
Helpline: 020 7403 5969
Address: c/o THT Counselling, 111–117 Lancaster Road, London W11 1QT
Internet: www.tht.org.uk

National Association of Bereavement Services provides information on bereavement services.
Telephone: 020 7709 0505
Address: 20 Norton Folgate, London E1 6DB

British Humanist Association can provide information and help with non-religious ceremonies.
Telephone: 020 7079 3580
Address: 1 Gower Street, London WC1E 6HD
Internet: www.humanism.org.uk

In addition to the above the **Government's website** www.Direct.gov.uk has information on practical matters and useful links to other agencies and sites.

BLIND VETRANS ASSOCIATION